The A–Z Guide to Common Habits

Also by Ann Gadd

The Girl Who Bites Her Nails and the Man Who Always Sighs: What Our Habits Reveal About Us

Finding Your Feet: How the Sole Reflects the Soul

Climbing the Beanstalk: The Hidden Messages Found in Best-Loved Fairy Tales

all published by Findhorn Press
www.findhornpress.com

The A–Z Guide to Common Habits

Overcoming Them Through Affirmations

Ann Gadd

FINDHORN
Press

The right of Ann Gadd to be identified as the author of this work has been asserted by her in accordance with the Copyright, Designs and Patents Act 1998.

ISBN 978-1-84409-100-3

First published in English by Findhorn Press 2007.

A CIP catalogure record for this title is available from the British Library.

Edited by Magaer Lennox. Cover design by Damian Keenan. Interior design by Thierry Bogliolo.

1 2 3 4 5 6 7 8 9 10 11 12 13 14 13 12 11 10 09 08 07

Published by

Findhorn Press
305a The Park, Forres IV36 3TE, Great Britain
Tel +44(0)1309-690582 • Fax +44(0)1309-690036 • eMail info@findhornpress.com

www.findhornpress.com

Table of Contents

Introduction

If I hit you on the head with a plank, you would initially feel *physical* pain. This would be followed by an *emotional* response because you would understandably feel angry at what I had done. You may also worry that I might repeat the assault. Later, while trying to figure out why a normally calm person would react in such an unreasonable manner, you may try to understand the *mental* reason for my action: you may wonder if I'd had a tough day and if I'd really meant to hit you on the head. You may also wonder whether I was actually a violent person who'd previously suppressed my true nature. You may take this even further by exploring the *spiritual* aspects of your now sore head. Were you being karmically repaid for similarly biffing someone in your previous life? Were you reaping what you had sown, by having negative attitudes or actions in this life?

One physical action affects the three higher levels of your being. The same effect occurs with our habits, only this time in reverse: your *spiritual*, *mental* and *emotional* states create your *physical* habit. Devouring chocolate by the slab, or eating your yummy de luxe tuna sandwich too fast, may be physical behaviour, but these habits have deeper causes. And unless we understand the spiritual, mental and emotional reasons for our habits, we'll continually try to give them up, with little or no positive results.

As an alternative practitioner, I see every day how the subtle non-physical aspects of ourselves affect our physical bodies. After many years of treating clients, I am still amazed by how this relationship between the physical and the non-physical, and how understanding the true nature of our behaviour, can bring about significant positive change and empowerment. The need to indulge in our physical habits is removed if we work toward removing the thoughts and emotions that have created those particular behaviours. Releasing ourselves from our habits means that we can live more satisfying lives now. And when we release negative forms of behaviour, the universe replaces the 'gap' with something infinitely more rewarding, be it a metaphysical experience, a greater sense of well-being or a new and exciting opportunity. I know this process works because I have witnessed it many times and applied this process to my own life.

I tended to find a hundred-and-one things I had to do before I went out, which inevitably made me late for my appointments. In truth, I wasn't really interested in the work I was supposed to be doing and I was expressing my resentment for the task by subconsciously sabotaging the occasion or appointment from the very beginning. When I was able to identify this, I was able to let go of the need to seek approval by always saying 'yes', and I started saying 'no'. I also accepted that if I, by my own free will, accepted an appointment or invitation, then I was not honouring my integrity if I was late. By empowering myself to say 'no' and drawing clear boundaries for myself and others, I felt much less stressed and I stopped feeling resentful.

This book will not cure your habit any more than reading the instructions on a box of headache pills will cure your headache. However, it will help you understand why you do what you do. Armed with this understanding, you will be better equipped to eradicate the thought patterns that no longer serve you. You can become your own healer, and in doing so, access the inner power that comes with being balanced on all levels of being.

We are often blind to the unpleasant aspects of ourselves: we don't want to delve into our own shadow natures for fear that what we discover will be hard to deal with. Instead, we resist becoming more conscious of who we are because once we reach some form of self-realization we are invariably pressed to change our thoughts, actions or emotions. For most people, change is not appealing, which is why we often choose to avoid, rather than confront, the negative aspects of ourselves.

It is not easy to accept responsibility for our lives. However, if we do, we empower ourselves to change what we don't like about ourselves and our lives. We become co-creators of our own reality, rather than passive victims of circumstance.

Using this book will take courage as well as the belief that you can change your habits by becoming aware of your thought patterns and then altering them. Changing these *out*comes necessitates a journey *in*ward. By releasing those thoughts and emotional patterns that do not serve you, you step closer to your Divine potential. I trust that this book will guide you on your way.

What causes a habit to develop?

Why do you bite your nails, have to grab a cup of coffee before you can start the day, procrastinate, draw the same image when you doodle, check that the car door is locked at least twice, play with your hair, or battle to be punctual?

We all have habits, even if we don't think that we do! Ask someone who lives or works with you and they will inevitably reveal at least one behavior that you repeat.

Habits develop as a form of stress release. We create expectations for our lives from our own life experiences. When these expectations are not met, we become disappointed and this creates stress, which we relieve by performing certain habits. Different expectations and beliefs create different habits or outcomes. However, despite causing an initial release of stress, our repeated habits can also incur guilt, which then increases our stress levels, which we once again reduce by performing the habit. As the spiral of negative behaviour increases, so does our stress.

This book will help you identify which emotional circumstances or patterns of thinking trigger your stress. The tendency has been to work the opposite way round: we feel guilty about our habits without understanding why they started in the first place. We put a bandage on the surface of the wound, without first cleaning out the emotional muck – and then we wonder why the wound (or habit) and the resulting guilt remain. Guilt, by its nature, holds us in the past, unlike fear that projects us into the future. So it becomes impossible to fully live in the present when we are feeling guilty about an action from the past. This, I believe, is why stopping a habit can be so difficult.

Habits can also be great helpers. Because of their repetition, negative habits constantly remind us that something in our psyche is causing us emotional distress. If we work with our habits, we can release many of the patterns of thinking that could lead to more serious illnesses over time.

The word 'habit' originates from *gabei*, which means 'to grab hold of'. Think of your habits as your helpers, grabbing hold of you and saying, 'Hey, we have a problem here'. By taking notice of our habits, we can avoid continuing down a road that could lead to a more serious threat to our health or psyche in the future. Ignoring our habits, and the lessons they can teach us, is equivalent to walking down a busy freeway with a blindfold on.

Children and habits

In a family, a young child may develop a habit for which there appears to be no emotional cause. Sometimes, however, children pick up on their parents' suppressed emotion and behaviour and express it themselves. Parents need to be aware of this and should take a long and courageous look at themselves to see whether the child is not simply expressing the suppressed emotions of a close adult.

For instance, a toddler may bite their nails. As nail biting is a symptom of suppressed anger, the parent would need to ask whether they're not suppressing their own anger. The parent may be experiencing the inner tension that builds when we don't say what we really feel. For instance, an unexpressed desire for approval in the relationship between the parents could result in the parent internalizing their anger. In situations of threat, our nails could be used to claw and attack. Biting our nails, our means of attack, is the physical expression (or habit) of the emotional angst that's created when we don't claw at the people who anger us. The parent may not be biting their own nails, but the tension of their suppressed anger is felt by a sensitive child who then acts out the habit.

It is accepted wisdom in metaphysical philosophy that all individuals are intrinsically linked, within the immediate family as well as within the global human family. What one person does affects the whole family, the society they live in, which in turn affects the country and all of creation. Being aware of this may help us to work not only with our own habits, but also those of the people close to us. If our partner or child has a certain habit, what is this mirroring in us? Our relationships provide potential for learning and our children's habits can be important tools to understanding ourselves.

How to recognize and differentiate between a habit, an addiction and Obsessive Compulsive Disorder

We can define a habit as a repeated automatic response to a specific situation. It is a practice we do regularly and that we find difficult to give up. As such, it may involve addictive behaviour: our response to a certain event or emotion can be the desire to take an addictive substance, such as a cigarette or a double Scotch. Smoking is certainly a habit, but because it involves a substance which we crave, it is also an addiction.

The word 'addiction' is most commonly, though not exclusively, used to indicate the compulsive need for a particular substance. A habit refers to the more general practice of repeating behaviour, whether that involves a physical substance, an emotional response or a mental attitude. So although all addictions are habitual, not all habits are addictions.

Obsessive Compulsive Disorder (OCD) also involves habitual behaviour but differs in its cause and extent. OCD may involve obsessive thoughts that are compounded by disturbing thoughts and images. The practice of a particular behaviour neutralizes these fears. For instance, you may fear a fatal illness from contamination by touching certain things or people. You may compulsively clean all the surfaces in your house to stop the feared fatal illness or disease from occurring.

OCD is found in only two to three per cent of the population and usually starts in early adulthood. Commonly, recurring thoughts or impulses create extreme levels of anxiety and stress. The thoughts may be violent (as in the desire to harm someone), sexual (as in the overwhelming desire for inappropriate sexual behaviour) or fearful (as in being afraid of certain circumstances or the results of actions). A fearful thought could be: that no matter how many times you check the oven is off, it is actually not off and will result in the house burning down.

The most common form of the disease requires the sufferer to perform a habit or ritual in order to stop certain events from occurring. Disturbing thoughts may be suppressed or eradicated by performing certain habits such as *checking* that a stove was switched off, a door locked or that accounting figures are accurate. The case of the stove may involve watching it for an extraordinarily long time before being satisfied that it is actually switched off. *Repeating* becomes a compulsion when a habit must be repeated in order to prevent the initial fear from occurring. *Arranging* of certain items in a very specific way, *hoarding*, extreme *slowness* while performing everyday tasks, uncontrollable *worrying* thoughts, *fear* of having a bowel movement, *fear* of urinating in a public toilet and specific phobias may all, when experienced in excess, be indicative of OCD.

This book is about habits: it is important to distinguish between the habit of checking a few times that your front door is locked and behaviour that reaches such debilitating extremes that it is impossible to work and maintain a normal lifestyle. OCD may involve a ritual or habit, but because of its compulsive aspect, it requires professional intervention.

How affirmations work

How can saying a phrase or sentence actually change our lives? The idea seems a little far-fetched but not when we examine how our subconscious functions. The subconscious has enormous power and can be compared to a powerful, but very dim giant. It acts on instructions, without any thought as to why it's doing what it has been instructed to do and has no ability to analyze a thought or emotion. The subconscious will not question any message it receives, but like a soldier it'll do exactly what it's told irrespective of what the outcome or effects may be on the individual.   Let's say the message given to the subconscious is: 'You can't make a living from art'. This message may have been planted in the subconscious through:

- Witnessing: e.g. as a child watching someone else who painted and who faced poverty.
- Hearsay: being told as a child by a parent or teacher that all artists are poor and only become famous after their deaths.
- Experience: having your art rejected and consequently affirming to the self that you're not a good artist and therefore can't make a living from art.

One day your art does start being accepted. Consciously you're thrilled. Subconsciously the message that's sitting there though is: 'You can't make a living from art'. So the subconscious sets about making sure that you can't. You may sabotage your success by ignoring your intuition when it comes to what and how you should paint, or letting any rejection confirm the basic belief that you have about art and earning a living. Your conscious mind is like a brainy nerd - all thoughts and little power to act. So no matter how many times you tell yourself that you can be successful, your far more powerful subconscious is acting to make sure that it follows the instructions implanted in it, even if that occurred many years ago. It's a case of the mighty giant versus the puny nerd.

Another example might be overcoming feelings of a lack of self-worth, which manifest in the habit of being highly critical of others. No matter how much we tell ourselves consciously that we are worthy of being loved, if the subconscious programme says that we're unworthy of love, it'll win the battle and manifest situations, which will confirm our lack of worth and give us reasons to dislike ourselves even more.

The purpose of affirmations is to reprogramme the subconscious. Telling yourself that: 'I make a comfortable living from art' or 'I am worthy of being loved for who I am' with the right amount of input starts to reprogramme the subconscious. The more you repeat the phrase, the deeper it's implanted. You can even make a tape of the repeated affirmation and play it to yourself while sleeping, where it can get through to the subconscious without the interference of the conscious mind.

The conscious mind will instill doubts and fears in the process. The more you can bypass the conscious mind, the more effective the reprogramming of the subconscious will be. This is why it's best to repeat the phrase often, to the point of it becoming a sort of mantra.

Any other ways you can use to programme your subconscious, such as drawing a picture of your desire or writing reasons why you want to change, as well as rituals such as burning a piece of paper on which you have written the old thought, symbolically inform the subconscious of the change.

Affirmations and present time

Another aspect to be aware of is that the subconscious is extremely literal. If your affirmation is: 'I want to lose weight', then you are informing your subconscious that you want to constantly exist in a state of *wanting* to lose weight and it will comply happily. When you say: 'I am thin', you inform the subconscious that this is the state you desire right now and it'll once again start to comply.

Another aspect of creation is that to manifest something, we first have to create the thought or its astral matrix before it occurs physically. The more specific we are the better the chance of the outcome being what we wanted. As there is no time in the astral plane of being, when we create something we need to create it as if it's already happening. Consequently we always use present time when doing affirmations. This may seem hard at first as your busy conscious mind will be telling you this is all a hoax and it hasn't happened. Acknowledge it and act in spite of it.

Creators

We, being the microcosm of the macrocosm that is God/the Divine (or whatever other term works for you) are creators. It's the true nature of God and therefore is our Divine inheritance, to create. We are extremely powerful creators; most of us just don't realize it. When we tap into this understanding nothing is impossible.

Personally I've found this ability to be an enormously powerful process. Yesterday I had breakfast with a top art gallery owner, did a midday lunch interview about my previous book and went on to the opening of an art exhibition of work by my husband and myself, which was almost a sell-out. A couple of years ago when I was struggling to get my first book published and selling only a handful of paintings a year, this would have seemed impossible. It's through experiencing my own process that I know that we can create the lives we choose and this includes dropping negative habits.

Hoping and knowing

Success with affirmations comes from being in a state of knowing rather than hoping. The more you hope something will happen the more you create the potential for doubt that it won't. So live in a state of knowing. Say your affirmations and then stand back from them - drop expectation and hoping and live in the calm knowing that it will occur. Simply through your thoughts, in one sense it has already.

Integrity and affirmations

There is another aspect to affirmations - integrity. Now most of us believe we have integrity insofar as we would not steal or deliberately mislead someone. However when it comes to personal integrity i.e. keeping our word to ourselves, few of us succeed. In fact if you start to monitor just how often you break your word to yourself, (always with the best of reasons and excuses) it can be quite an eye-opener. Things such as: 'I'll go to the gym three times a week'; 'I won't eat junk food'; 'I won't have more than one glass of wine'; 'I will write that email today'; and 'I will clean out the fridge' are all things we might say and yet seldom do. That may seem harmless, however from a creating perspective it is harmful.

Why? Simply because we are programming our subconscious with the belief that we're not as good as our word - we lack impeccability, and that means when we tell our subconscious something that we want to happen it treats it with the same disdain as it would if we told it we're not going to procrastinate any longer. By doing what you say you're going to do, when you say you are, in spite of whatever occurs or simply because you don't feel like it, you're letting your subconscious know that what you say happens. It then acts accordingly. So work with issues of integrity, it'll strengthen your ability to create whatever it is you want, from giving up smoking to loving yourself more.

What does it mean to be out of balance?

All our dis-ease comes from an imbalance in our system, which we attempt to balance. It can be likened to a pebble dropped in a pond – the further away from the centre, the bigger the waves become, or a see-saw, where the further away from the middle we are the bigger the ups and downs we experience. The further away we are from being centred or balanced, the bigger the emotional/mental waves/see-saw effect we create, which naturally causes us to live more stressful lives. These two poles of ourselves are likened to the elements of fire (masculine principle) and water (female principle). Too much fire and we carry excess energy, anger and resentment; too much water and we're tearful, depressed and unable to motivate ourselves, or we may see-saw between them. Being balanced then would be to balance these two elements within us resulting in a state of peace or tranquillity. At its essence this is what alternative healing is about. The more in balance we are the more empowered we are, and the more empowered we are the more what we say as an affirmation manifests.

How to use this book

Having found your habit in the A-Z listing, read through the explanations given and see which resonates with you, likewise with the affirmations. Your own emotional reaction – be it anger, denial, a feeling of 'Oh yes!' – is usually an indication that you have found the clue to the emotional cause of your habit.

Although you might find information about your habits illuminating, remember that others may not want to have their emotional 'stuff' exposed and may find your explanations of their behavior threatening and invasive. The safest rule is not to venture opinions or insights unless you are specifically asked to do so. Not everyone chooses to become more conscious in this way and we have to be mindful and respectful of that. Working to release our issues takes courage and perseverance and is not always very appealing. When working with others, do so with love, compassion and a complete absence of judgement.

You need to have compassion for yourself too. Recriminations and guilt will only keep you stuck. Having understanding and surrounding yourself with forgiveness and compassion will assist you through the process. Remember we are all here to grow; whatever patterns you have developed were created to assist you in your learning. Let go of blaming yourself and allow yourself to move on in love.

Carolyn Myss, author and metaphysical teacher, said in a workshop

I attended that 'Your biography becomes your biology'. The more you are able to recognize that your thought patterns and beliefs have a direct effect on your physical body and its reactions (your habits), the more you empower yourself to alter those thought patterns and beliefs that no longer serve you. This process becomes one of authentic empowerment. More importantly you move from the archetypal role of victim, where you feel disempowered to do anything about yourself or your circumstances, to victor, assuming full responsibility for all aspects of your life.

A—Z Listing

Habit	Mental/Emotional issue	Affirmation
Alcohol binges	Belief that we deserve some reward for what we're having to experience. Imbalance of fire (anger), which we attempt to soothe by the addition of water.	*I express myself. I am empowered. I am in balance. I reward myself in ways that are beneficial to my body.*
Animal Hoarding ----------See Hoarding: Animals		
Bedwetting	Releasing fear, anxiety, and sorrow, also anger.	*I am courageous and feel safe. I can express how I feel.*
Belching/burping	Not wanting to assimilate all that is happening.	*I create time for myself. I relax when eating. I digest experiences.*
Belittling:		
• **Others**	Feeling inadequate. Deep-rooted fear of partner leaving.	*I am worthy of being loved. I respect myself and others.*
• **Ourselves**	Needing others' approval to look good. Fear of our authentic power.	*I approve and love myself. I step into my power.*

Habit	Mental/Emotional issue	Affirmation
Biting:		
• Nails	Holding onto our anger. Wanting to claw at someone. Internalizing resentment.	*I express myself freely. I love myself enough to say what I feel. I release resentment and anger.*
• Objects	Needing to relax. Taking life too seriously. What do we really want to get our teeth into? A way of repressing our anger.	*I have the courage to communicate what I believe in. I release my aggression.*
• Parts of the body	Angry with self. A situation that is eating away at us.	*I choose to release my anger and confront the situation that makes me angry/unhappy.*
• Pencils/pens	A situation that is eating us up. The need to make a decision.	*I deal with situations and make decisions easily, trusting in my higher self to guide me.*
Blushing	Shame. Feeling exposed. Having feelings (often sexual) that we want to hide.	*I accept all aspects of my body, my feelings and my sexuality.*

Habit	Mental/Emotional issue	Affirmation
Boredom	Expecting others to stimulate us. Lack of creative connection.	*Life is full of excitement. All of life is an adventure to be explored.*
Boundaries:		
• **Lack of**	Poor grounding. Security issues. Lack of sense of self. Living in fear. Often history of abuse.	*I feel safe and secure. I let go of the need for others' approval. I stand up for myself.*
• **Rigid**	Lack of trust in life. Ruled by our fear. Afraid of change.	*I trust and feel safe. I feel vital and alive. I let go of feeling insecure and vulnerable.*
Bragging	Desperate need for acceptance and approval. Feeling inadequate.	*I love and approve of myself as I am.*
Breaking things	Frustration. Repressed anger for the person whose possessions we're breaking or a specific task we don't want to do.	*I honour my own free will. I can express myself freely.*

Habit	Mental/Emotional issue	Affirmation
Breath:		
• **Holding**	Tension. Not wanting to fully experience life. Restricting ourselves. Expecting the worst. Fear of letting go. Fear of independence.	*I have complete faith and trust in the process of life. I willingly receive all life has to offer. I breathe freely. I do not let others smother me.*
• **Fast/shallow**	Fear, nervousness and anxiety creating stress. Not wanting to fully engage with life. *I am open to receive. I am relaxed.*	*I live in faith and release fear. I absorb and participate in life fully.*
----------**See also Hyperventilating**		
• **Sighing** ----------**See Sighing**		
• **In through closed lips**	Sucking in what we really want to say. Holding back, usually anger or vengeance. Holding back venom.	*I accept others completely, even if their behaviour does not match my expectations.*
Bullying	Low self-esteem. Belief that relationships are power struggles. Often have experienced shame and abuse at home.	*I respect the will of others. I am worthy of love. My power comes from within. I nurture myself and others.*

Habit	Mental/Emotional issue	Affirmation
Bumping:		
• **Into people**	Wanting to be noticed. Needing attention. Not grounded. Confused.	*I am connected to mother earth.* *I am focused.*
• **Into objects**	Not grounded. Confused. Disorientated. Emotional confusion.	*I think and feel clearly.* *I know where I am going.*
Burping: ----------See Belching		
Bus: Always missing	Failing to move forward in life or sabotaging the desire to.	*I move forward with ease in my life.*
Busy: Need to always be	Avoiding feelings. Not wanting to admit or confront certain issues. Belief that self-worth is based on worldly achievement.	*I simply need to be. That is all.* *I am all I need to be. I value all that I am.*
Caring: For others not self	Codependency. Problems with receiving. Martyrdom Giving as a means of control. Denial of pleasure.	*I am open to receive. I value who I am.* *I do not need to suffer to be of worth.*

Habit	Mental/Emotional issue	Affirmation
Cars:		
• **Driving fast**	Avoidance. Escapism. Self-sabotage. Need to take risks in order to feel fully alive. Reacting without thinking first. Driving ambition to feel fully alive. Driven A-type personality[1]. Driving ambition.	*I am powerful as I am. I am responsible, reliable and always act with complete integrity towards myself and others. I have self-discipline.*
• **Driving far too slowly**	Wanting to control the speed at which change is occurring. Procrastinating.	*I more forward with ease.*
• **Driving recklessly**	Self-sabotage. Questions right to be alive. Belief that we're invincible. Difficulty relaxing. Belief that adrenalin rush is the only way to feel fully alive.	*I feel safe and secure. I have a right to be alive. I feel fully alive just being.*
• **Polishing frequently**	Very aware of the physical self. Need to look good.	*I give love and attention to my physical, emotional, mental and spiritual self. I do not need others' approval.*

Habit	Mental/Emotional issue	Affirmation
Checking repeatedly:		
• **Doors are locked**	Insecurity related to lack of boundaries or others respecting them. Feeling vulnerable.	*I trust. I feel secure within myself*
• **Handbag to see if purse is still there**	The need to affirm that we're secure. Insecure in issues such as relationships, finance, sexuality.	*I feel safe and secure in all areas of my life.*
• **Weight scale**	Belief that the physical self is the true self. Blaming our weight on the reason we're not happy.	*I am so much more than my body. Perfection is a state of being as opposed to a physical state. I am perfect just the way I am.*
Chewing: Gum	Avoiding making decisions. Chew things over as a way to avoid acting. Not wanting to really digest issues/life.	*I confront life passionately. I accept my life.*

Habit	Mental/Emotional issue	Affirmation
Chewing:		
• **Too little**	Not wanting to absorb all that is happening. Avoiding digesting details. Not breaking down issues into digestible pieces.	*I can see and accept the whole situation clearly. I embrace all parts of my experience.*
• **Too slowly**	Focusing on controlling the details and avoiding seeing the whole. Decision and deliberation as opposed to action and experience.	*I experience the wholeness of life. I balance action and deliberation.*
Chocolate: Eating excessively		
	Seeking love/comfort/intimacy. Desire for nurturance.	*The universe loves, nurtures and supports me. I am worthy of love and complete acceptance.*
Clapping	Building energy levels. Way of increasing energy.	*I am an energetic, powerful being.*

Habit	Mental/Emotional issue	Affirmation
Cleaning excessively:		
• Body	The belief that we're somehow dirty, either in our thoughts or what has happened to our body, or what we've been made to believe about ourselves or our sexuality.	*I am at ease and peace with my physical self. I am a spiritual being, experiencing a physical incarnation. I forgive myself and in doing so, purify and cleanse myself.*
• Car	Wanting to look good to get the approval of others, often because we don't really approve of ourselves. Needing validation for our physical selves.	*I am perfect and I love myself just the way I am. I only need approval from myself.*
• House	Wanting to make everything appear to be OK, when it is not.Having some control when we feel out of control.	*Everything is perfect just the way it is. I give up feeling a victim and step into my power.*
Clumsy ----------See Bumping		
Coffee: Drinking excessively	Needing constant stimulation to overcome anxiety and fear. Putting ourselves in a fight as opposed to flight mode. Low energy. Low self-esteem causing constant stress. Needing to boost self.	*I feel safe and secure. I love and approve of myself. I am fully capable of dealing with whatever occurs in my life.*

Habit	Mental/Emotional issue	Affirmation

Collecting:

- **Cars (big) different models**

  Projecting many aspects of ourselves to feel less vulnerable. Wanting to ensure that we always have a way to get/be ahead.

  I do not need external power to affirm my internal power. I move through life with joy and ease.

- **Cars (big) same model**

  Projection of external power. Often lacking internal power. Wanting to ensure that we always have a way to get/be ahead.

  I do not need external power to affirm my internal power. I move through life with joy and ease. I welcome a variety of experiences in my life.

- **Books**   Desire for knowledge and personal growth. Can be ego-related need to affirm our knowledge.

  All the wisdom of the universe lies within me. By studying the axiom 'as above so below', knowledge is revealed to me.

- **Cars (miniature)**

  Diminishing the self and with it our potential. Holding onto lots of disempowering beliefs.

  If I have the idea, I have the potential.

Habit	Mental/Emotional issue	Affirmation
Collecting (continued)		
• **Clowns**	Avoiding confronting issues in our lives. Clowning around as a way to avoid going into emotional pain.	*The true self is the higher self. I allow myself to feel, so that I can heal.*
• **Masks**	Not being true to self. Developing an outward expression of self that masks the true inner one as a means to feel good about self.	*I express the truth of who I am. I am worthy of being loved for who I am.*
• **Miniatures**	Wanting to feel in control. Attempting to reduce problems to the point they can be manipulated.	*I let go of fear. I enjoy a challenge. I confront areas of my life where I have problems.*
• **Souvenirs**	Attempting to hold onto experiences.	*I flow through life with ease. I let go of one experience in order to create the new.*
• **Stamps**	Attempting to keep the world in an ordered fashion. Desire to make a good impression.	*I enter into the joy of life without limitations and expectations. I am good enough as I am.*
• **Watches**	Desire to control the passing of time. Need or desire to keep a watch on ourselves or others.	*I have plenty of time. Time is only real on the physical plane. Everything happens the way it should.*

Habit	Mental/Emotional issue	Affirmation
Computer:		
• **Cyber slacking**	Avoidance. Procrastination. Boredom with actual task on hand.	*I love and enjoy the work I do. I am always in my integrity. I release my pattern of procrastination.*
• **Gaming**	Avoidance. Escapism. Feeling disempowered. Avoiding communication.	*I express myself freely. I recognize my worth. I release the pattern of avoidance within me.*
Coughing: Nervously	Fear of being heard. Fear of expressing ourselves honestly.	*I express myself truthfully, and freely. I communicate openly.*
Counting:		
• **General**	Attempting to keep track of things. Insecure. Control issues.	*I release the need to control life. I accept things as they are.*
• **Number plates**	Feeling out of control. Attempting to create order in our lives.	*I trust the process of life and feel secure. I accept the perfection in life, just as it is.*

Habit	Mental/Emotional issue	Affirmation
Criticizing	Dislike of self. Self-hatred. Often carrying guilt issues.	*I truly love myself. I accept myself and all I am as being part of the Divine creation. I forgive myself and let go of the past.*
Cross-dressing	Being forced to deny the feminine in all of us. Suppression of feminine nature. Having to appear macho in order to be approved of.	*I embrace and accept the feminine side of myself. I integrate my male and female aspects. I approve of all aspects of myself.*
Crossing legs	Protecting our sexuality. Feeling slightly ashamed about our primal urges.	*I lovingly embrace my sexuality as a vital aspect of myself. I am open to receive.*
Crying:		
• **Often**	Sadness masking anger. A fire and water imbalance. Crying (water) as opposed to venting anger (fire). Feeling compassion and connection for others and their pain on a deep level.	*I express my anger and resentment. I forgive myself and others.*
• **Never**	Detaching from our feelings. Intellectualizing how we feel. Lack of compassion for self.	*I allow myself to express my feelings freely. I have compassion for myself. I am comfortable with my feelings.*

Habit	Mental/Emotional issue	Affirmation

Defecating: Unable to do so except at home

| | Fear of letting go. Holding onto our stuff in front of others. Afraid to express our true selves in the company of others. | *I release my anger and sadness. I let go of emotions that do not serve me. I approve of myself and don't need the approval of others* |
| **Dominatrix** | Desire to humiliate, control and dominate, often as a way to revenge childhood trauma and own childhood feelings of not being in control. | *I release all past hurt. I am compassionate towards myself and others. I create the life I want. I let go of the need to control others.* |

Habit	Mental/Emotional issue	Affirmation
Doodles/Placement:		
• **Top of page**	Free-thinking. Often spiritual interests. Ethereal. Energetic. May also feel that our ideas are more important than those we're listening to.	*I am well grounded. I listen openly and without judgement to the ideas of others.*
• **Centre of page**	Extrovert who wants to be the centre of attraction. Can be self-centred. Desire for freedom, expansion and non-restrictive environment.	*I am free and flow with the experiences of life. I express myself freely. Others' approval is immaterial because I approve of myself. I honour and love myself.*
• **Left side of page**	Relates to the past and issues to do with females or inner female. Whatever is drawn will point to which issues. May indicate fear of the future.	*I let go of the past and move forward with joy. I surrender to life and accept what is.*
• **Right side of page**	Relates to the present and male or inner male issues. Desire to communicate emotions to others and self. Desire for action.	*I am fully present at all times. I take the required action. I communicate with myself and others truthfully and openly and drop the need for approval.*

Habit	Mental/Emotional issue	Affirmation

Doodles/Placement (continued)

- **Bottom of page** Practical, earthy or depressed and feeling burdened. — *I release the illusion of my burdens. I am empowered and uplifted.*

Doodles/Line pressure:

- **Light lines** Sensitive. Afraid to make our mark. Need for approval. Low self-esteem. — *I move beyond my fears and perceived limitations. I approve of myself and freely express my true self.*

- **Medium lines** Balanced. Good sense of self.

- **Heavy lines** Suppressed aggression. Desire to express. — *I release my anger. I am at peace. I forgive myself and all those who I believe have wronged me.*

- **A combination of line types**

  Insecurity. No sense of self or direction. Adaptable and open to change. The meaning will depend on what is depicted in the doodle. — *I create purpose and meaning in my life. I am open to change.*

Habit	Mental/Emotional issue	Affirmation
Doodles/Types:		
• Random unstructured	Desire to express ideas. Often frustrated desire to be creative	*I give up seeking the approval of others. I am a creative, artistic being and I express my creativity.*
• Repeated lines	Methodical and ordered. Unfocused and scattered. Bored.	*I embrace change. I create focus and integrity in my life.*
• Vigorous lines	Energetic and impatient.	*I am relaxed. All that I require manifests at the appropriate time. I live in clarity and peace.*
• Wavy lines	Strong or deep emotions. If lines are calm and peaceful: feminine, receptive, rhythmic emotional state. A dreamer. Musical ability.	*I flow with the river of life. I surrender to experience. I have an inner balance of fire and water elements.*
• Zig-zag lines	Life is experienced as harsh – at the cutting edge. Desire for safety and comfort away from the cutting edge.	*I am safe, nurtured and protected. I rely on Divine wisdom to be my guide.*

Habit	Mental/Emotional issue	Affirmation
Doodles/Types (continued)		
• **Large complex doodles**		
	An artistic nature wanting to express ideas rather than listen to others' ideas.	*I am an artist. I am able to express creatively all that I desire.*
Doodles/Symbols:		
• **Arrows**	Ambition. Masculine desire.	*I live in knowing rather than hoping. All that I need comes to me. I am open to receive.*
• **Boxes**	Contained and need for structure. Self-imposed limitations. Restriction. Feeling stuck. Unsure of the way ahead.	*I move forward with ease. I am able to change. I experience life as full of opportunity, joy and excitement. I trust my inner wisdom to guide me.*
• **Dots**	Need to join the dots, i.e. gain insight into a situation. Scattered emotions and instability.	*I am conscious of all the patterns in my life. I am totally clear and focused in my thinking and feeling.*

Habit	Mental/Emotional issue	Affirmation
Doodles/Symbols (continued)		
• **Eyes**	Feeling scrutinized. Needing to see something clearly. The ego in charge.	*I do not need to suppress how I truly feel in order to be approved of. I need answer only to the Divine and my own conscience.*
• **Houses**	Represent the self. Small houses: feeling insecure. No windows: desire to withdraw from the world due to unhappiness.	*I am safe and secure. I have complete trust in the world and share joyous interaction with others. I am a Divine spark.*
• **Ladders**	On a spiritual path or desire to succeed.	*I am a success. I can achieve whatever is in accordance with my higher purpose.*
• **Maze**	Seeking solutions or a way out of a situation. Confusion from complicating issues.	*I see a clear path ahead for my life. I am totally clear in my thinking. I confront any decisions I have been avoiding.*
• **One's signature**	Undeveloped sense of self.	*I love myself as I am.*
• **Web**	Feeling trapped or feelings of connectedness to all things.	*I am free to make choices.*

Habit	Mental/Emotional issue	Affirmation

Eating:

- **Bland food** — Fear and difficulty with anything new. Desire to remain in control.

  I am open to experience. I live in trust. I let go of fear and feel safe and secure.

- **Mushy food** — Avoiding getting in touch with own aggressive feelings. Desire to avoid any challenges. Avoiding experiencing life.

  Being authentic with my feelings is a way of stepping into my authentic power. I am open to experience all the joy life has to offer.

- **Salty food** — Desire to increase male aspects of self or left-brain thinking.

  I am balanced and in harmony with all aspects of myself. I think clearly and analytically when I desire.

- **Spicy food** — Seeking excitement and stimulation.

  I live in a world full of exciting experience.

- **Sweet food** — Desire for love and nurturance. Feeling unworthy of being loved.

  I am worthy of love. I love myself.

- **Chocolate**
  ----------See Chocolate: Eating excessively

Habit	Mental/Emotional issue	Affirmation
Eating (continued)		
• **Too much**	Lack mentality. Replacing the intimacy you crave with food.	*I am clear, conscious and focused. I have a deep and intimate relationship with myself and others.*
• **Too fast**	Guilt in taking nurturance for yourself. Not feeling worthy.	*I deserve love and acceptance. I have compassion for myself.*
• **Too slowly**	Attempting to control others who are eating with us. Attention seeking.	*I let go of fear. I am worthwhile simply being as I am.*
Exaggerating	Feeling inadequate. Low self-esteem. Desire for others' approval.	*I approve of myself and let go of the need for the approval of others. I am worthy of being loved for who I am.*

Habit	Mental/Emotional issue	Affirmation
Exercise:		
• **Don't**	Domination or need to control others leaves no energy left for exercise. An imbalance between male and female aspects of self.	*I let go of the need to control others. I am balanced between doing and being.*
• **Over**	Escapism. Using exercise to avoid facing other issues.	*I do not need to achieve in order to feel good enough. I confront and work through all my emotions.*
Exhibitionist	Craving for attention and confirmation of self. If sexual: a desire to have one's masculinity/ femininity affirmed. Often history of abuse. Lack of boundaries for self and sexuality.	*I need only approve and love myself. I love my masculine and feminine sides. I am a man/woman in the truest sense of the word. I have clear boundaries for myself and my sexuality.*
Explaining: Excessively	Creating a story to avoid accepting responsibility or to confirm to ourselves that we're right.	*I give up the need to be right. I accept full responsibility for my life and how I act, think and feel.*

Habit	Mental/Emotional issue	Affirmation
Eyebrows: Plucking	Wanting to control how we express ourselves.	*I trust and feel safe in the world. I express my feelings openly.*
Scratching	Irritation with others. Indecision as to how to express what we feel. Wanting others to see what is a problem for us.	*I am able to confront openly what is irritating me. I communicate openly what I feel.*
Farting: Excessively	A desire to let off steam/anger. A desire to cause a stink.	*I express what I feel. I feel love for those around me. Joy replaces anger.*
Fault-finding	Self-dislike. Not approving of self.	*I let go of my need to be perfect. I let go of the need to be right. I love myself. I rejoice in the uniqueness of each person.*
Fearful/anxious	Not trusting in the process of life. A victim mentality.	*I feel safe and secure. I am powerful.*

Habit	Mental/Emotional issue	Affirmation
Fetishism	Little self-esteem. Inability to relate to peers. Possibly a traumatic exposure to sex.	*I am able to communicate in a relaxed and open manner to all people. I release past trauma. I am worthy of intimacy and love.*
Fiddling: Hands playing with objects		
	Not saying what we really feel. Boredom. Frustration often at not being understood or wanting our ideas to be accepted.	*I express myself freely. My ideas and feelings are always heard. I am enthusiastic about my ideas and so are those I share them with.*
Fingers: Drumming ----------See Tapping: Fingers		
Forgetfulness	Feeling neglected. Resistance to doing something we don't want to do. A life full of 'should' and 'must'.	*I am loved and appreciated. I live according to my truth and not the will of others.*
Frottage	Fear of emotional intimacy. Seeing people as objects.	*I am worthy of wonderful and intimate relationships. I have compassion for myself and all others. I am confident and love myself.*

Habit	Mental/Emotional issue	Affirmation
Gambling	Addiction to risk. Idealized view of life. Denial.	*I let go of the need to experience risk in order to feel alive. I see reality totally clearly. I am truthful to myself.*

Good: The need to always look good /acceptable /approved of

	Suppressing the real you in order to please others. Denial of real self. Avoiding confronting the shadow self.	*I love all of who I am. It is immaterial what others think of me. I drop looking good and express my truth.*
Grinding: Teeth	Desire for revenge. Anger at perception that another has taken advantage of us. Wanting to harm another who we perceive has harmed us.	*I forgive others who I perceive have harmed me. I let go of the past. I realize that whatever occurs is a gift of understanding and gives me the opportunity to gather light.*
Gulping: Food	Taking life in too quickly. Belief in lack. Not trusting in abundance.	*I am abundant. I live in a world of abundance. I enjoy each precious moment of my life.*

----------See also Eating: Too Fast

Gum: Chewing
----------See Chewing: Gum

Habit	Mental/Emotional issue	Affirmation
Hair:		
• **Brushing constantly**	Stimulates mental faculties and enhances power. Desire for clarity.	*I think clearly and with focus. I am centred in my authentic power.*
• **Gel**	The need to control our thoughts and appear to be thinking with ease.	*I trust and let go of the need to control. I live in faith not fear.*
Hair/Pulling:		
• **Eyebrows**	Afraid of expressing our true thoughts. Frustration at controlling how we express ourselves to please others.	*I believe in myself and my ideas. I express myself truthfully and with clarity. I drop the need for the approval of others.*
• **Head**	Intense frustration. Not feeling others are listening or accepting our ideas. Not wanting to connect with higher guidance. The desire to please others.	*I live in peace. I communicate with integrity and truth. I am in constant connection with my higher self and live my life according to this guidance. I approve of myself as I am.*

Habit	Mental/Emotional issue	Affirmation
Hair/Pulling (continued)		
• **Pubic**	Shame of sex. Afraid of expressing our sexuality. Pulling our hair out over sexual issues or the power others hold over them.	*I am relaxed and in harmony with my sexuality. I am in my sexual power.* *I make the choice to stop others abusing me in any manner.*
Hair		
• **Shaving pubic**	Desire to revert to child-like state. Desire to be taken care of and to return to innocence.	*I am always safe and protected.* *I love my inner child.*
• **Sucking**	Need to draw in power. Need to feel energized. Need to be nurtured. Feeling insecure.	*I am safe and secure. I step into my authentic power. I feel loved and protected.*
• **Twirling**	Enhance our personal power. The desire to twist someone around our finger, i.e. have power over them.	*I am in my power and as such let go of the need to control and manipulate others.*
Head-banging	Anger and frustration at not being understood. Irritation at not getting anywhere with our desires or needs.	*I live in acceptance. I take responsibility for who I am. I use the energy of my anger to make the changes I need to in my life.*

Habit	Mental/Emotional issue	Affirmation
Hearing: Not doing so even though nothing physically wrong		
	Not wanting to hear what others are saying. A desire to shut out the world. Avoiding being nagged.	*I have a choice in all matters of life. I am open to and embrace life. I confront and transform what does not serve me.*
Hoarding:		
• **Animals**	Hero/martyr archetype. The need to feel more important/self-righteous than others. Need for sympathy from others. Extreme need for control.	*I value myself for who I am not what I do. I do not need to suffer or allow other creatures to suffer in order to be of worth. My specialness comes from the Divine spark that is in me and all other human beings.*
• **Objects**	Insecurity. Fear of letting go. A lack mentality. Attachment. Not trusting the process of life. Control issues.	*I know that whatever is released will be replaced with something better. I clear out all my old patterns to make way for the new.*

Habit	Mental/Emotional issue	Affirmation

Holidays (Vacations):

• **Always getting ill on one**

| | Living under huge stress. Not feeling we deserve a break. Punishing the self. Relaxation releases control and all the buried stress. | *I deserve to have a break. I am worthy even when at rest. I am always relaxed and at peace.* |

• **Not being able to defecate on one**

| | Not being able to release the past and live in the present. Fear makes us hold on. Needing to feel in control. | *I live in present time. I let go of my fear and trust the process of my life. I enjoy the challenge of new experience. I gather more light with each new experience.* |

• **Not taking one**

| | Fear of change. Fear of experiencing the new. Not wanting to let go of control. Wanting to believe that we are irreplaceable in the workplace to affirm sense of self. Belief that we are only worthy doing and not just being. | *I embrace change. I grow from all new experiences. I am. That is all I need to be. I honour myself for who I am and not what I do.* |

Habit	Mental/Emotional issue	Affirmation
Holidays (Vacations):		
• **Diarrhoea**	Fear. Feeling out of control. Inability to hold onto new experiences. Fear of change.	*I trust that the new experiences are there to serve my growth. I embrace each experience as an opportunity to learn and become more conscious.*
Hyper-responsible	Overtly sacrificing. Feeling over-protective, often as a way to avoid being responsible for our own true selves.	*The only adult person I need to be responsible for is myself. The only responsibility I ultimately have is to the Divine and my own conscience.*
Hyperventilating	Not wanting to take in life fully. Feeling restricted. Not trusting life. Flight or fight mentality. Extreme stress. Expectation that what can go wrong will. Feeling a victim of circumstance.	*I let go of fear. I have choices and as such am empowered to act. I expect only what is needed and good for me to occur. I am free and absorb life with love and passion.*
Insomnia	Afraid of what might occur. Stress. Worry about the future. Not wanting to go into our subconscious. Anxiety. Drinking to extreme as an attempt to overcome stress and fear.	*I breathe deeply and peacefully. I let go of my fear and the need to control the outcome. I live in trust. I live in the joyous now. I let go of the concerns of the day and relax completely.*

Habit	Mental/Emotional issue	Affirmation
Interrupting	Desire to dominate and control. Often we don't want what our partners say to reflect badly on us. The need to be right.	*I feel secure within myself. I listen more than I speak. I do not need to be approved of by anyone other than myself.*
Internet Surfing: ----------**See Cyber-slacking**		
Keys		
• **Always losing**	Not wanting or feeling capable of finding the solutions to problems. Losing our way.	*I have a clear direction for the future. In my life there are no problems, only solutions.*
— **House keys**	Losing sense of self or self-esteem. Or unable to find solutions relating to the self.	*I trust my own intuition. I am open to change. Everything will work out for the highest good.*
— **Car keys**	Losing means of getting ahead or unsure of how to get ahead.	*I move through life with ease. I am clear in the direction I want to take. New and exciting opportunities come my way.*
— **Office Keys**	Losing ability to find solutions in the workplace.	*The work I do supports me physically, emotionally, mentally and spiritually. There is always a solution. I am not blinded by the fear of change.*

Habit	Mental/Emotional issue	Affirmation

Keys (continued)

• **Needing to lock everything**

Seeking to block access of others to our inner selves. Wanting to lock ourselves away to avoid experiencing life and through fear of rejection/hurt.
[If it is only certain things then this will relate to what those things symbolize.]

I am free and open to experience, life and others. I only experience loving relationships with others. I am fully accepted for who I am.

• **Forgetting to lock**

Issues with boundaries. Allowing others free access to ourselves to the point that we may not respect who we are. Not sure where we end and others begin.

I am contained. I respect my boundaries and those of others.

Kleptomania

Addiction to thrills. Anger at society in general. Seeking revenge on the social system.

I live in balance. I release the need for thrills to make me feel alive. I feel tolerance and forgiveness towards others.

Habit	Mental/Emotional issue	Affirmation
Knees: Rubbing	Finding it hard to be submissive and compliant with the wishes or demands of others. Afraid to bow down. Anger at having to be compliant, usually with peers. If left knee only: a woman. If right knee only: a man. Anger at not being able to move forward.	*I let go of the need to be in control. I surrender with ease. I am always in my truth and integrity with others. I do not allow any person to rule me. I am free to do what is appropriate for me.*
Laughing: Too loudly	Wanting others to see us as light-hearted. Wanting to feel we belong. Masking insecurity.	*I lovingly accept who I am. I am a microcosm of the Divine macrocosm. It is safe for me to be my true self.*
Legs: Tapping ----------See Tapping: Legs		
Loosing things	What is missing in our lives? Look at the actual items and see what they symbolize to us. Then ask ourselves why we may not want to hold onto them. Are we feeling lost in life?	*Whatever I need comes to me. Nothing is ever truly lost, simply replaced. I find direction and meaning in my life*
----------**See also Keys: Losing**		

Habit	Mental/Emotional issue	Affirmation
Lying	Not having respect for self or others. Feeling inadequate and needing to boost self. Lying to others in order to avoid confronting the truth about ourselves. Blaming others. Fear of not receiving approval from others. Belief that deceiving others makes us superior to them.	*I live with total integrity to myself and others. I approve of who I am. I value myself sufficiently to want to remain in my truth. I am always speaking and acting in truth and integrity, which enhances my sense of self and my spiritual development. I am fully responsible for myself and my life.*
Make-up: Wearing too much	Wanting to mask our true selves and emotions. Not liking the self. Afraid that people will not love us if they see the real person.	*I love myself. My radiant true self is my Divine self. It is enough to simply be who I am.*
Manipulating: Others	Feeling afraid and using manipulation in an attempt to control those around us to feel more secure. Control issues.	*I feel safe and secure. I respect the will of others.*

Memory ----------**See Forgetfulness**

Habit	Mental/Emotional issue	Affirmation
Moral righteousness	Fear of being wrong, so our way has to be right. Need to be right. Lack of true joy in our lives. Perfectionism.	*I respect the views and choices of others. I let go of the need to be right. I accept that what I feel is perfect is not necessarily a view that is shared by others. I let go of the expectation that everyone should behave in a way that I feel is perfect.*
Moustache: Playing	Drawing attention to our authority and masculinity. Drawing in warrior energy.	*I am a peaceful warrior and consequently empowered.*
Nail-biting	Repressed anger towards another/others/self. Internalizing frustration because we're afraid that by showing how we really feel others will not approve of us. Belief that expressing or having angry feelings is not 'nice'. Sabotaging our defence instead of protecting ourselves.	*I am able to express how I feel. I let go of the belief that expressing anger is wrong. I use the fiery anger of my feelings to transform my life. I establish appropriate boundaries for myself.*

Nail: Picking or biting of skin around nails

Habit	Mental/Emotional issue	Affirmation
	Tension and fear relating to feeling secure and protected. Fear gnawing away at us. Feeling vulnerable, which causes stress.	*I am always safe and secure within myself. I confront and then let go of what makes me afraid.*

Habit	Mental/Emotional issue	Affirmation

Nicotine ----------See Smoking

Nose:

- **Picking** — Wanting to take life in freely and openly. Problems with self-worth. Picking away at what frustrates us about not having our achievements recognized. — *I value who I am. I list and acknowledge all I have achieved. I breathe in joy.*

- **Playing with** — The need for recognition and appreciation. — *I value who I am. The recognition from others is no longer important to me.*

- **Sniffing** — Holding back from expressing issues that have upset us. Subconsciously wanting others to recognize our pain. — *It is OK to express how I feel. I acknowledge all that I have been through and now move on. I transform my pain into pleasurable experiences.*

- **Sneezing** ----------See Sneezing

Habit	Mental/Emotional issue	Affirmation
Obsessions with:		
• **Appearance**	The need for others' approval. The inability to express ourselves openly and freely. Low self-esteem.	*I let go of the need to please others. I am an aspect of the Divine and consequently perfect as I am. I express myself.*
• **Celebrities**	Not feeling good about who we are. Living life through other people's achievements as a way to avoid actually doing anything with our own life.	*I create the life I have always wanted for myself. If I think it, I can become it. I am not afraid to make the changes I need to in my life.*
• **Shoes: Having many pairs**	Unsure of what steps in life we need to take. Experimenting with many different roles. Taking on too many roles in life. Scattered energy.	*I decide on a path to take and follow it. I am focused in what I want to achieve.*
Oracles: Constant need to consult	Not trusting our own intuitive abilities. Seeking validation of our intuition. Hoping that the oracle will tell us what we want to hear as opposed to what the truth is.	*I trust in my intuitive self. I know rather than hope that my inner voice has all the answers I need. I do not allow my fear of change and the truth to cloud the answers I receive.*

Habit	Mental/Emotional issue	Affirmation
Organizer: Needing to organize everyone and everything		
	Need for control. Being in charge keeps insecurities at bay. Feeling disempowered and needing to control others in the belief that this will empower the self.	*Everything is perfect as it is. I need only have self-control. I drop the need to dominate others. I am energized and feel fully alive.*
Over-eating ----------See Eating		
Overweight	A desire for intimacy. Replacing the need to be loved and nurtured with food. Belief in lack (of love, nurturing, compassion etc). Carrying others or own emotional stuff.	*I receive all the love and nurturing I need. I release all codependent relationships and only have relationships with equal giving and receiving. I have close and intimate relationships with others.*
Paraphilia		
	Unable to have appropriate intimate relationships with peers. Belief that sex is dirty. Seeing others as objects rather than feeling individuals. Fear of vulnerability in a relationship. Often reverts to childhood fantasies and experiences because it feels safer.	*I let go of my fear of rejection and enter into deep and loving relationships with other adults. I express the beauty, love and sharing that sex can potentially be.*

Habit	Mental/Emotional issue	Affirmation
Passive resistance	Codependent relationships. Fear of speaking up and saying what we feel, yet brewing on issues resentfully. Sabotaging another as a way of revenge because we feel unable to stand up for ourselves.	*I live in integrity and truth. I let go of resistance and repression and am honest with myself and others as to how I feel. I value and honour myself.*
Perfectionism	The need to be and make everything right at the expense of our own happiness. The belief that our way is the right way. What is perfect? Each person has a different view and who is to say whose view is right?	*I let go of the need to be right and in doing so, open the doors to a happier state of being. I value myself for who I am, not what I do.*

Habit	Mental/Emotional issue	Affirmation
Piercing:	Pain of feeling isolated and misunderstood. Rebelling. Emotional pain made physical.	*I accept myself as I am. I express how I feel and release the hurt of the past.*
• Brows	Wanting to draw attention to our pain.	*I acknowledge my hurt.*
• Gums	Feeling insecure.	*I feel secure and loved.*
• Lips	Unspoken pain.	*I express my feelings.*
• Nipples	Pain of not feeling nurtured.	*I love and nurture myself.*
• Nose	Needing recognition.	*I am recognized and loved for who I am.*
• Penis	Sexual pain.	*Sex is a loving and beautiful way of expressing myself.*
• Tongue	Unable to express the pain we feel.	*I release all that is bitter in my life.*

Habit	Mental/Emotional issue	Affirmation
Piercing (continued)		
• **Vagina**	Sexual pain.	*Sex is a loving and beautiful way of expressing myself.*
Pimples:		
• **Squeezing**	Releasing anger and inner conflict often to do with sexual issues.	*I embrace my sexuality. I am a sexual and sensual being. I release any negativity I may have towards my sexual expression.*
• **Squeezing someone else's pimples**	Desire to help someone else release their emotional issues. Can also be related to sexual release.	*I cannot do the work of releasing for another; I can only facilitate their process.*
Playstation **See Computer: Gaming**		

Habit	Mental/Emotional issue	Affirmation
Procrastination	Resisting change. Avoidance. False optimism. Self-deception. Viewing things as we would like them to be rather than as they are. Crisis management and the adrenalin-pumping feeling of having won against the odds. Perfectionism. Fear of failure. Convincing ourselves that we're 'too busy'. Taking on a job we believe is below or above our capabilities. Not feeling equipped to handle the job. Boredom with what we're required to do. Passive resistance. Trying to look good and please others by not saying no and taking on more than we can handle.	*I welcome change. I am totally clear and truthful in all I do and say. I do not need a crisis in order to feel of worth. Either nothing is perfect or everything is perfect as it is. I let go of my fear that something won't be perfect. The work I do is in alignment with my soul's purpose. I learn to say no. I let go of delay and confront and release all issues and emotions as they arise, so that I can truly live in the present.*

Habit	Mental/Emotional issue	Affirmation
Punctuality		
• **Being late**	Needing to control the situation or the person. Living out of our integrity. Devaluing another's worth. Ego as opposed to integrity.	*I let go of the need to control others. I value each person and understand that if I do not value them I do not value myself.*
• **Being early**	Insecurity. Establishing control of the situation before those that threaten or the situation that threatens occurs.	*I trust and feel secure in the world. I let go of the need to control, it only makes me feel more insecure.*
• **Late: Because of doing unrelated things before we go**	Resistance to actually going where we have to go. Perhaps we said Yes when we wanted to say No, so as not to cause offence or because our work dictates that we have to be somewhere we would rather not be. Doing things beforehand that make us late is a form of passive resistance.	*I let go of the words 'should' and 'must'. I learn that it is alright to say no. I do not sacrifice my integrity to please another.*

Habit	Mental/Emotional issue	Affirmation
Quarrelling	Inner conflict and turmoil that reflects on the outside world.	*I am at peace with myself.* *I release anger and frustration.*
Reading: The end of the book first	Needing to control the outcome. Is this a mirror in our life?	*I trust that life will unfold perfectly for me and the lessons I have chosen to learn.*
Religious fanaticism	Fear originating from a lack of trust of self and others. The need to be right. Fighting external demons rather than confronting your own. Desire to belong.	*I trust life. I respect other's beliefs.* *I understand that there are a number of paths to the Divine.*
Repetition: Of words or phrases	Usually the word or phrase relates to how you would like to be. Wanting to emphasize to another that you are this way.	*I approve of myself. I let go of the need for the approval of others. I am perfect as I am.*

Habit	Mental/Emotional issue	Affirmation
Right: The need to be	Control. Self-esteem problems. Fear of others recognizing that we are not perfect. The need for perfection because deep down we feel flawed.	*I live in joy and happiness. I understand that there is no right or wrong, simply degrees of understanding.*
Risk taking	Needing to come close to death to feel alive. Questioning right to be here. Forcing ourselves to do courageous acts to overcome self-doubt.	*I feel fully alive every moment of the day. I am free of limiting beliefs and fears.*
Sabotaging: Self	Low self-esteem. Fear of taking responsibility for ourselves and our lives. Belief in not being good enough and therefore destined to failure.	*I am courageous. I embrace change. I step into the full potential of my being.*

Habit	Mental/Emotional issue	Affirmation
Scratching:		
• **Bum**	Irritated at not releasing an issue. Something we should have released is still sitting with us and causing anger or frustration.	*I let go of the past. I release my frustration, irritation and anger.*
• **Crotch**	Do we have a sexual itch, i.e. need for sex, which we cannot pursue? What about sex is causing us frustration or anger?	*I embrace my sexuality. I release all painful sexual experiences. I find deep fulfilment through exploring my sexuality.*
• **Ears**	Irritation at what we're hearing. Not wanting to listen to what irks us. Stimulating our ability to listen.	*I am open to listening and receiving. I listen to my inner communication.*
• **Eyebrows** ----------see Eyebrows: Scratching		
• **Feet**	Irritation with ourselves for not moving forward. Irritation with parents or parental figures. Frustration at not understanding an issue. Itching to change.	*I move forward with ease. I let go of the need for parental approval. I have deep levels of understanding and use this to alter my life appropriately.*

Habit	Mental/Emotional issue	Affirmation
Scratching (continued)		
• **Hair on head**	Needing to stimulate thinking. Something that irritates us to the point of wanting to pull our hair out often because we're afraid to express what we really think or believe in case it offends.	*I am a genius. I am open to hearing the answer so any question I ask will be answered. I think clearly. I express the truth of what I think or believe.*
• **Skin**	Irritated with having to interact with the outside world. Something that is frustrating or irritating you. Repressing your aggression. Holding back from expressing something.	*I allow my aggression to surface so that I can work with the problem and release it. I express what has been irritating me below the surface. I am at peace with myself and others.*
• **Toes**	Are our own or others' thoughts or beliefs making us frustrated? Are our ideas not being well received? Do we want or need to stimulate our thinking?	*All the information I need comes to me. I think clearly and my ideas are well received. I accept that there are degrees of understanding and my beliefs may not always be approved of and I am OK with this.*

Habit	Mental/Emotional issue	Affirmation
Self-harming	Self-hatred. Deep-rooted self-esteem issues. Dealing with extreme emotional pain in a physical way. The emotional pain is often a result of abuse in childhood.	*I express how I feel to others. I have unconditional love, compassion and acceptance for myself. I accept that I was abused but choose not to continue to abuse myself.*
Shop-aholics	Belief that security comes from possessions. Feeling disempowered emotionally. Seeking to empower ourselves materially.	*I am all I need to be. I have self-worth. I am a powerful Divine spark. I am safe and secure always.*
Shop-lifting	Entitlement. Thrill-seeking. A way to provide for ourselves or our habits. Peer approval. Feeling beyond or above society's rules. Lack of accountability. Emotional pressure and anger relieved by stealing. Sabotaging our position through lack of self-worth. Depression and anxiety.	*I respect the rights of others and their property. I let go of my anger and fear. I respect the boundaries of society as I enforce my own. I value myself.*

Habit	Mental/Emotional issue	Affirmation
Shrugging	Attempting to shed responsibility. Resenting being made to feel responsible.	*I accept that only by being responsible will I find true freedom. In being responsible for my life I empower myself to manifest it.*
Sighing:		
• Long in-breath, short out-breath	Frustration and anger. Holding back what we want to say. Manipulating others through wanting to make them responsible for how we feel.	*I accept responsibility for all my emotions. I can choose to remain angry or release it. I let go of the need to control others.*
• Long out-breath	Releasing emotions. Reaching for relaxation and peace.	*I release my stress and arrive in the peace of now.*
Skin-picking	Extreme dislike of self. Lack of self-love. Making our inner pain visible. Picking away critically at ourselves. Trying to be perfect. Emotional stress. Boredom.	*I love and feel compassionate towards myself. I am perfect as I am. I let go of the illusion of perfection and accept myself, loving the way I am.*

Habit	Mental/Emotional issue	Affirmation
Sleep:		
• **Talking**	Expressing subconsciously what we've consciously held back. Stressful issues from the past that remain unresolved may be worked through in sleep. Internalizing our emotions. Fear. Stress.	*It's OK to express how I feel. I am aware of how my past issues influence my present. I now choose to release the fear and pain surrounding them.*
• **Walking**	Stress, anxiety and conflict in the surrounding. REM behaviour disorders[2]. Lack of definition between astral and physical planes, which can be a result of previous trauma experience. Depression. Flight from a perceived attack.	*My true state is tranquillity. I address all my fears and overcome them. I trust my higher self to keep me safe and secure. I address any trauma in the past and receive the help I need to work through the issue.*

Habit	Mental/Emotional issue	Affirmation
Sleeping:		
• **On back with arms at side**		
	Surrendering and letting go of the need to control. Trusting. Independent.	*I feel safe and at peace.*
• **On back with hands above shoulders**		
	Open and trusting. Open to share our feelings.	*I feel empowered and relaxed.*
• **Foetal position**		
	Vulnerable and needing nurturing.	*I am safe and the universe supports me.*
• **On the side with legs straight**		
	Open. Trusting (sometimes too trusting) in male related areas if on left side and female if on right side.	*I let go of feeling vulnerable.*

Habit	Mental/Emotional issue	Affirmation

Sleeping (continued)

• **On the side with arms out-stretched**

Reaching out. May be needy.

I trust that there will always be assistance when I need it. I am able to give to myself.

• **On stomach**   Protective of our emotions. Feeling emotionally vulnerable. Can appear friendly, loud and outgoing, but may mask a sensitive nature.

I feel safe and secure in the world.

• **Not being able to:** ----------See Insomnia

Habit	Mental/Emotional issue	Affirmation
Sleeping positions: Couples		
• **Front-to-back**	Intimacy and love.	*I cherish the intimacy and love I find in the world.*
• **Back-to-back**	Trust and feeling safe in the relationship.	*I thank the universe for all aspects of the relationship that I am in. I become more conscious of myself and others through this relationship.*
• **Legs touching**	Independent but moving forward in the same direction.	*I am grateful for the balance between independence and intimacy that I experience in my relationship.*
• **Buttocks touching**	Intimacy, trust and independence in the relationship.	*I bring this relationship into balance by bringing myself into balance.*

Habit	Mental/Emotional issue	Affirmation

Sleeping positions: Couples (continued)

   • **Opposite sides of the bed**

| | A need for our own space. Seeking separation. All relationships are a mirror of the balance within ourselves and between our male and female aspects. | *I have a joyful, fulfilling and intimate relationship with myself. I am balanced between my own male and female aspects. I move from a relationship of codependence into one of choice and acceptance.* |

Sleeping: With a pet

| | Desire for intimacy which we feel unable to receive from another person. Non-threatening closeness. | *My relationships are balanced between giving and receiving. I experience intimate relationships with myself and others. I open myself up to receiving the love I deserve.* |

Sleeves: Pulling up to elbows

| | Needing to assert self with others. Wanting to expose ourselves to new experiences. Wanting to show our capability. | *I know that I am a powerful being therefore I do not need to demonstrate this power. I know I am capable and do not need to prove this to others.* |

Habit	Mental/Emotional issue	Affirmation
Slumping: Body posture		
	Not wanting to stand up for ourselves. Low self-esteem. Not feeling worthy.	*I stand in my power. I approve and love myself. I am a Divine spark. I act in spite of my fear.*
Smoking	Wanting to remove ourselves from the reality of an emotion or situation by creating a smokescreen. Taking in life in a toxic way. Difficulty breathing in joy. Imbalance between feeling and thinking.	*I am totally clear in seeing the truth of my life. I am balanced between my water and fire elements and consequently my heart and head. I take in life with joy. I freely express how I feel.*
Sneezing	Getting rid of our aggressive emotions or irritation towards another.	*I release my anger towards others, recognizing that the cause is anger towards myself. I am at peace with myself and others.*
Sniffing	Holding back sadness and not expressing it. Wanting to be recognized. Sadness at not being acknowledged. Not recognizing how upset we really are.	*I release the sadness and open myself to joy. I recognize my Divine nature. I am open to experience and fulfilment.*

Habit	Mental/Emotional issue	Affirmation
Snoring	Fearing change. Anger at ourselves for not changing, towards others and circumstances who we feel are forcing us to change. Subconscious blocking of new experiences. Stuck.	*I freely breathe in every wonderful moment of my life. I accept change as part of life and embrace the new experiences it brings. I create the life I want.*

Song:

• Singing, humming

	Stress releasing. The sound frequency is an attempt to soothe our anxiety through the vibration. Using sound to bring us into balance.	*I am always calm and serene. I am in perfect balance.*

• In our heads

	Listen carefully to what the words of the song are saying. Does this have any relevance to us? What were the circumstances when we first heard the song? Can we relate the emotions to emotions we are feeling now?	*I am always conscious of the messages that the universe is giving me to assist me in self-realization.*

Habit	Mental/Emotional issue	Affirmation
Speaking:		
• **Deep tone**	Masculine power. Strong. Grounded.	*I use the grounded power I have to assist those who are not grounded so they can feel connected.*
• **Garrulousness**	Avoiding true feelings. Nervous. Attempt to release emotions while avoiding experiencing them. Need for attention. Wanting to draw from others. Control. Communicating with others to avoid communicating truths to ourselves.	*I listen more than I speak. I am open to insight. I use the insights I gain to understand the negative patterns I create so I can consciously stop repeating them. I draw from within all the power I need. I am wise and use my experiences to connect with this inner wisdom.*
• **Loudly**	Need to dominate and gain attention because we feel insignificant.	*I release the need to control. I am filled with energy. I realize that my loudness comes from feeling small–I now choose to feel empowered.*
• **High pitch**	Seeking control or domination without any authentic power. Imbalance of fire and water. Ungrounded and scattered.	*I ground myself. I am centred and fully in my internal power. I speak clearly with resonance and authority.*

Habit	Mental/Emotional issue	Affirmation

Speaking (continued)

- **Monotone** — Fear and resisting change. Trying to control the situation. Lacking personal power. Afraid to fully experience all aspects of the self. — *I embrace all change–it is an opportunity to grow. The more I allow myself to change, the more I can experience and the more fulfilled I become.*

- **Mumbling** — Fear of being heard. Fear that what we say will not meet with approval. — *The vibration of my words creates positive results in myself and others. I speak confidently, clearly and with deep power. I am heard.*

- **Nasally** — Needing recognition. — *I do not need outside recognition to validate myself. I am worthy just being. I step into my full potential.*

- **Repetitively** — Belief that we're not being heard. Wanting others to hear us. — *I listen with full attention in order to always be heard.*

- **Softly** —
  - Feminine power where softer is more powerful.
  - Fear of being heard. Lack of self-esteem and therefore afraid that what we say will not meet with approval.
  —
  - *I embrace my full power as a woman.*
  - *I approve of myself, always. I am free to express my thoughts and approval irrespective of whether others approve of me.*

Habit	Mental/Emotional issue	Affirmation
Speaking (continued)		
• **With mouth full of food**		
	Not digesting issues before we act on them. Leaping into things without thinking. Imbalance in hearing and listening.	*I listen more than I speak. Before I speak, I take the time to consider what I am about to say and decide then if it is relevant.*
• **Whining**	Disempowered. Manipulative. Needy and demanding.	*I am able to translate what I feel into words easily. I find ways to express what I feel through creativity. I am the only authority figure in my life. It's safe to be me.*
Spitting	Releasing emotions, (often anger as in spitting mad), that we've held back.	*I communicate freely. I let go of my anger and the fear or sadness that lies beneath it.*

Habit	Mental/Emotional issue	Affirmation
Stroking: Part of our body	Desire to soothe and relax. What specifically we want to soothe will depend on which part of the body, e.g. our leg would be our desire to move forward as in wanting to be calm about how we proceed.	*Peace is at the essence of my being.*
Stuttering	Fear of disapproval usually from an authoritarian father or parental figure. Extreme sensitivity. Shamed by others. Lack of self-worth. Unable to express ourselves for fear of upsetting others.	*I approve and love myself. I am balanced between my fire and water elements. I am always in my integrity towards myself and others. I value myself. I express my thoughts and feelings freely.*

Habit	Mental/Emotional issue	Affirmation
Sucking:		
• **Cheeks in**	Holding back cheekiness or outspoken comments.	*I express how I feel constructively.*
• **Lower lip**	Holding back from saying what we want to.	*I drop the need for others' approval.* *I express what I have repressed.*
• **Hair**	Wanting to draw in more power to feel secure.	*I feel grounded, safe and nurtured.*
• **Shirt/clothing**	Insecurity and feeling unprotected.	*I am not afraid. I am loved and nurtured by all of life. I am protected.*
• **Sweets**	Wanting sweetness in our lives.	*Life is sweet and I am open to experience it.*
• **Thumb**	Need to feel safe and nurtured.	*The Divine universe nurtures me.*

Habit	Mental/Emotional issue	Affirmation
Sulking	Passive aggressive behaviour. Domination through manipulation. Withdrawal rather than engaging in confrontation. Feeling disempowered and so seeking to control others.	*I give up trying to control others. I realize that my need to control is fear-based and I choose to move beyond my fear. I step into my authentic power. I clearly express my needs.*
Swearing	The words used indicate how we perceive the world, ourselves and others and the anger we feel about this. For example 'shit' equates to 'worthless', 'fuck' equates to 'violent, insensitive, debased and lacking love', 'wanker' equates to 'unable to experience wholeness, isolated and self absorbed'.	*I always have the power to choose. I choose always to see all that is beautiful, loving and divinely nourishing in my life. I release my anger and blame and reach acceptance.*
Talkative ----------See Speaking: Garrulousness		
Tantrums	Childlike inability to deal with the world not being the way we believe it should be. Frustration at not being understood. Codependent expectations. Feeling victimized and living in blame.	*I release all expectations that others should make me happy. I am responsible for my own happiness and life. In order to be heard I need to learn first how to listen.*

Habit	Mental/Emotional issue	Affirmation
Tapping:		
• **Legs: Both legs**	Frustration at not being able to move ahead in the direction we would like to. Perceiving that others are holding us back. Impatience. Agitation over the slowness of others. Energy build-up.	*I move forward through life with ease and harmony. Everything happens in perfect time. The only limits are those I put on myself.*
• **Left leg**	To do with female issues within self which hold us back or actual women who appear to thwart our progress.	*I am in touch with my empowered female aspect. There are no limitations. I allow myself to progress and move in the direction I need to go in.*
• **Right Leg**	To do with male issues within self. Our male aspects relate to taking action. If we're afraid or feel limited, we feel stuck and tension builds. May also be seen as actual men who are hindering our progress.	*I let go of all fear in taking the direction that I need to go in. What I perceive as being others holding me back is simply a projection of my own fears, which I now choose to release.*
• **Fingers**	Wanting to grasp an idea or express one. But feeling frustrated that we can't or that others won't get what we're trying to convey. Wanting to come to grips with an issue, but believing we can't because of the petty details. Overlooking the details because we're moving too fast. Frustration over details.	*I grasp new ideas with ease. I take the time to plan projects before rushing into them. I see the big picture but realize I need to work on the details to be successful. I only take on what I can handle.*

Habit	Mental/Emotional issue	Affirmation
Tattoos	Desire to create an outward persona because of insecurity within.	*I am perfect and worthy.* *I love myself as I am.*
Tea: Drinking excessively	Desire to calm ourselves and take stock. Desire for friendship.	*I am calmness. I meditate regularly.* *I connect on many levels with many people.*
Teeth grinding	Desire to attack or seek revenge on someone we perceive has harmed us. May not be conscious.	*I release all anger and revengeful thoughts. I see the lesson and personal mirror in all that has occurred and am grateful for what I have learned from the situation/person. I forgive myself and them.*

Habit	Mental/Emotional issue	Affirmation
Television:		
• **Compulsive watching**	Escapism hoping that the problem(s) will disappear by themselves. Not wanting to live life fully. Experiencing emotions in a distant way to avoid our own feelings/pain.	*I confront and release what is upsetting me. I release my pattern of avoidance. I feel in order to heal.*
• **Having it on constantly**	Wanting to shut out the reality of what is happening. Creating external noise to avoid inner turmoil.	*I am an expression of peace. I truly listen to my intuition and feelings.*
• **Not hearing another speak when it is on**	Avoidance. Passive resistance. Dominating through withdrawal.	*I drop the need to control. I express my anger and the emotions beneath it and acknowledge how I am feeling.*
Throat: Clearing	Nervousness in speaking our truth. Getting rid of any emotional content to do with what we have to say.	*I openly and calmly speak my truth.*

Habit	Mental/Emotional issue	Affirmation
Tics:		
• **Nervous:**	Fear and anxiety. Fear of failure. Desire to be controlled or to control. Problems communicating emotional issues. Need for approval. Insecurity.	*I succeed by simply doing. I lovingly approve of who I am. I feel secure and calm at all times, with all people and in all places. I express myself.*
• **Face**	Fear of facing-up to someone or something. Wanting to mask how we really feel.	*I confront all that is disturbing in my life and release the sadness, fear or anger that surround the issues/people. I express who I am and others love and appreciate who I am.*
• **Grunting**	Wanting to control our deep-rooted anger. The anger may be subconscious and so results in a primal, animalistic outburst. The harder we try to control it and pretend we're not angry the more it arises.	*I release my anger and acknowledge the pain, sadness and fear that lie beneath it. I let go of the need to please others. I clearly and truthfully express my own feelings.*
• **Head**	Not wanting people to see what is really going on inside us. Feeling a jerk. Hoping that through avoidance the situation will disappear.	*I am comfortable with who I am. I accept myself lovingly. I rejoice in being me. I see clearly the truth in my life.*

Habit	Mental/Emotional issue	Affirmation
Tics (continued)		
• **Shoulder**	Resisting feeling responsible for an issue or emotion– trying to shrug it off. Pretending something is not important to us when it is.	*I am only responsible for myself and the Divine. Compassion is I cannot carry the burden for others but feel compassion for them. So I allow others to help themselves. I acknowledge my hurt.*
• **Eye**	Avoiding seeing something clearly.	*I see clearly and intuitively.*
• **Touching others**	Wanting to connect with others. The desire for intimacy stemming from experiencing rejection of ourselves or our feelings.	*I am lovingly embraced by the universe. I am accepted and accepting.*
Tidying	The need for control. Belief that if all is perfect then our lives will be secure. Trying to create order when our physical or emotional life feels chaotic.	*There is Divine order in the universe even if it does not appear to be so. I feel safe and secure in the world even if things appear imperfect. I let go of the need to control and step into the wonderful world of acceptance.*

Habit	Mental/Emotional issue	Affirmation
Tobacco: Chewing	Wanting to feel calm. Desire to withdraw from digesting issues in our lives to feel happier about where we are; yet not dealing with them causes stress, which we relieve by chewing.	*I am conscious of all my feelings. I give up avoidance and embrace the reality that is my life, knowing I have the power to change things*
----------See also Smoking		
Toes: Playing with	Wanting to stimulate thinking. Desire to bring in clear, creative ideas. Wanting to be receptive.	*I am open to receive new thoughts, ideas and beliefs.*
Toilet training: Resistance	Wanting to have control. Feeling disempowered or powerless possibly because of feeling unheard, isolated or abandoned in some way.	*I am always listened to. I am not alone. I am empowered. It is safe for me to let go.*
Touching: Touching people while in conversation (not with a lover)	Needing to connect but feeling disconnected. Wanting to draw on the energy of others because we feel our energy is depleted. Lack of personal power. Lack of boundaries.	*I stand in my power. I create appropriate boundaries in order to affirm my power. I draw on the infinite resource of power in the universe.*

Habit	Mental/Emotional issue	Affirmation
Trainspotting	Need for control because of fear. Desire to be free yet needing discipline.	*I accept my fear and act in spite of it. There is no freedom without discipline.*
Trichotillomania: ----------See Hair: Pulling		
Tripping	Sabotaging our progress. Not feeling confident of the direction we have taken.	*I step into the world with confidence and trust that the path I have chosen is perfect for what I need to learn.*
Tugging trousers while arguing	Wanting to emphasize that we're in control or want to be, i.e. 'I wear the pants'. 'You must listen to me, I want to be dominant here.'	*I let go of the need to dominate. I am in my power and do not need to overpower another. Dominating is tiring work I free up my energy by letting go of the need to dominate.*
Twitch: ----------See Tics		

Habit	Mental/Emotional issue	Affirmation
Urinating: Constant need to		
	Needing to let go of fear. Insecurity or anxiety in the home. Fear of change. Too much going on emotionally. Need to release anger often at a parental figure. Not wanting to deal with or acknowledge emotions or events.	*I am always safe and secure. I release my emotions freely, having processed and acknowledged them. I bring awareness to how I feel. I live in tranquillity.*
Vacations: ----------See Holidays		
Voyeurism	Unable to relate confidently with our peers. Need for control. Emotionally repressed. Childhood abuse/ trauma that make us fear actual sexual contact. Gratification without being vulnerable.	*I accept my vulnerability. I release the desire to feel in control of others. I release the trauma of the past.*
Web surfing: ----------See Cyber slacking		

Habit	Mental/Emotional issue	Affirmation
Walking:		
• **Fast**	Goal orientated. Fiery energy. Wanting to escape the past. Feeling the need to achieve.	*I live and enjoy each precious moment of my life fully. I don't allow the goal to destroy the enjoyment of the now. I value myself irrespective of what I have achieved.*
• **Slowly**	Resisting change. Life feels tedious. Excess watery energy. Life has become an effort. Enjoying the moment.	*I am open to change. Life is one fantastic, exciting exploration.*
• **Avoiding pavement cracks**	Wanting to feel contained. Not wanting to step outside the box. Afraid of doing what we really want to do.	*I go freely wherever I want to go. I overcome my limitations to expand my sense of self.*
• **Dragging feet**	Not wanting to progress in life. Resistance to change.	*I move forward with ease. I enjoy every step of the way of my life.*

Habit	Mental/Emotional issue	Affirmation

Walking (continued)

- **Rigid body, with only legs moving**

  Inflexible. Fear of connecting with the physical body. Rigid belief systems.

  I let go of the need to control. I am open to the universe and all it has to offer.

- **With left foot turned outwards**

  Living for the future – not content with the present situation.

  I live totally in the present. I am content.

- **With right foot turned outwards**

  Living in the past. Allowing issues from the past or issues to do with men or our own masculine principle to hold us back.

  I release the past and live in the present moment.

- **With both feet splayed outwards**

  Needing direction in life or going in the direction we believe others want or demand of us.

  I find my own path in life. I am perfectly balanced and have my boundaries in place.

Habit	Mental/Emotional issue	Affirmation
Washing often:		
• Hands	Rejecting the way experience has touched us. Attempting to rid ourselves of what we've experienced or don't want to experience. Fear of reaching out to others. Not wanting to grasp what is happening.	*I am open to receive all the wonderful experiences life has to offer. I release the past negative experiences. I reach out to others.*
• Feet	Wanting to rid ourselves of the path we've had to walk. Letting go of experience. Wanting to start afresh. Washing away all the negative issues we've picked up.	*Each day is a new beginning for me. I release what no longer serves me. I step into the future with direction and positive purpose.*
Whistling a tune	Using sound to calm ourselves. Creating a relaxing rhythm. Can also be releasing tension over issues we would rather not speak about.	*I am peaceful and harmonious. I am able to air my feelings.*
Work-aholic	Issues with self-esteem – not feeling worthy unless we're achieving. Need to be right. Shame or domination in childhood.	*I am worthy simply being. I release my suppressed anger in a constructive way. I let go of the need for things to be perfect. I learn to relax.*

Habit	Mental/Emotional issue	Affirmation
Workshop-aholic	Belief that power lies outside of ourselves. Seeing the guru in everyone else but not in ourselves.	*I acknowledge that wisdom is learned through experience and recognition of our patterns. I cannot buy enlightenment.*
Yawning	Feeling depleted. Needing to draw in extra life force. Drained. Bored with the mundanity of life. Needing fire energy.	*Life is full of excitement. I am an inspired and creative being. I lovingly accept the new into my life. I am filled with fiery creative energy.*

Endnotes

[1] An A-type personality is someone who needs to be first and in control of others. They often have a need to be right about things or have the last word. They have a driving ambition and often will stop at nothing to satisfy their competitive demons.

[2] REM or Rapid Eye Movement is a stage in sleep that we all experience. It is the time when we're most likely to be dreaming. It is so called because the pupils move as if they're watching a film, even though the eyelids are closed.

Do you know of a habit that isn't in this book?
If so please send an e-mail to habits@findhornpress.com
and, if possible, Ann Gadd will get back to you with an explanation.
Your suggested habit might even feature in the next edition of the book!

Also by Ann Gadd

Are your habits driving you crazy? Are you sabotaging yourself through your unconscious, seemingly uncontrollable actions? Do you constantly lose your keys, procrastinate, bite your nails, battle to be punctual, snore, play with your hair, drink too much coffee or smoke 20 cigarettes a day…?

Most of us reading the above list would have identified with at least one of the examples, if not most of them! All these habits, together with many hundreds not listed, may be irritating or even detrimental to our health in the long term, but seem to ease our tension in the short term.

Why is habitual behaviour so intrinsic to our existence? Until now we have largely overlooked, denied or ignored our habits, yet as the mind-body connection becomes more understood, we have to acknowledge that there must be a connection between what we do physically and what we feel emotionally. *The Girl Who Bites Her Nails And The Man Who Is Always Late* offers unique insights into the reasons behind why we behave as we do. In looking at a whole range of quite common habits, involving the breathing system, the mouth, speech, sex, manipulative and harming habits, habits of children and of the elderly, etc., it becomes clear how our often-unconscious behaviour is a physical manifestation of an emotional state of mind.

Through their very repetition, learning how to understand and change or eliminate our habits is a great way of becoming happier, healthier human beings.

The Girl Who Bites Her Nails And The Man Who Is Always Late
Findhorn Press • ISBN 978-1-84409-073-0

Also by Ann Gadd

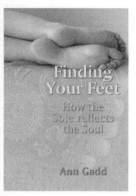

Ever wondered why you have crooked toes or bunions, or why your feet are hurting? Our feet are an amazing mirror to our physical, emotional, mental and spiritual imbalances... Addressed to both holistic professionals and those interested in finding out more about themselves, this illustrated treatment manual examines the mind–body connection in specific relation to the chakras and feet. Key issues and ailments are listed for each particular aspect of the foot, along with further explanations and case histories – including sections on overall shape, shoes, broken nails, and foot colour. Discover how the chakras are mirrored on the feet, learn about the five basic types of feet, about feet and Fibonacci, left foot and right foot and a lot more! The second part of the book reviews particular aspects of the foot such as:

- amputated toes
- ankle sprains
- arthritis
- athletes foot and other fungus problems
- bruises

- bunions
- burning feet
- calluses
- chilblains
- corns
- cuts

- footprints
- gout
- hairy toes
- hammered toe pads
- hammer toes
- splinters/thorns

- squashed toes
- nails (split/thickened)
- skin peeling
- smelly/sweaty feet
- swollen areas
- wrinkles

Finding Your Feet: How the Sole Reflects the Soul
Findhorn Press • ISBN 978-1-84409-081-5

Also by Ann Gadd

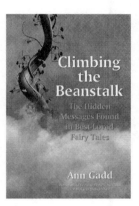

Revealing the secret truths found in classic fairy tales, this groundbreaking spiritual guide inspires readers to discover their own interpretations of the stories and recognize their sacred values when retelling them. A wide range of ancient fairy tales are analyzed both psychologically and spiritually, and the resulting guidance, insight, and hidden messages will offer a new perspective to readers who may have taken the fairy tales for granted. The book ultimately asserts that fairy tales' profound teachings are still relevant to human development and contemporary society, offering wisdom that should not be ignored.

Climbing the Beanstalk: The Hidden Messages Found in Best-Loved Fairy Tales
Findhorn Press • ISBN 978-1-84409-094-5

Books, Cards, CDs & DVDs that inspire and uplift

For a complete catalogue, please contact:

Findhorn Press Ltd
305a The Park, Findhorn, Forres IV36 3TE, Scotland, UK

Telephone +44(0)1309-690582
Fax +44(0)1309-690036
eMail info@findornpress.com

or consult our catalogue online (with secure order facility) on

www.findhornpress.com